WHEN YOU ARE DIAGNOSED
WITH A LIFE-THREATENING ILLNESS

DIFFICULT TIMES SERIES

*W*HEN YOU ARE DIAGNOSED
WITH A LIFE-THREATENING ILLNESS

JAN JOVAAG ANSORGE

Augsburg

MINNEAPOLIS

WHEN YOU ARE DIAGNOSED
WITH A LIFE-THREATENING ILNESS

Unless otherwise noted, scripture is from the Revised Standard
Version of the Bible, copyright © 1946, 1952, 1971 by the Division
of Christian Education of the National Council of the Churches
of Christ in the USA. Used by permission.

Large-quantity purchases or custom editions of this book are
available at a discount from the publisher. For more information,
contact the sales department at Augsburg Fortress, Publishers,
1-800-328-4648, or write to: Sales Director, Augsburg Fortress,
Publishers, P.O. Box 1209, Minneapolis, MN 55440-1209.

Cover Design by David Meyer
Book Design by Jessica A. Klein

Library of Congress Cataloging-in-Publication Data
Ansorge, Jan Jovaag, 1942-
    When you are diagnosed with a life-threatening illness / Jan
    Jovaag Ansorge.
    p.   cm.—(Difficult times series)
    ISBN 0-8066-4359-5 (alk. paper)
    1. Sick—Psychology. 2. Adjustment (Psychology) I. Title. II. Series
    R726.7 .A575 2002
    616'.001'9—dc21   2001053284

The paper used in this publication meets the minimum require-
ments of American National Standard for Information Sciences—
Permanence of Paper for Printed Library Materials, ANSI
Z329.48-1984. ♾™

Manufactured in the U.S.A.   AF 9-4359

06   05   04   03   02   2   3   4   5   6   7   8   9   10

✌ Contents ✌

✣ Introduction ✣

Throughout the seven years that I have had cancer, I have kept a journal. My journal has been useful in many ways. It serves as a record of treatments, side-effects, medications, instructions, and suggestions from my doctor or nurse. In it I also write questions that I want to ask my doctor, as well as questions that other cancer patients have for him (he is brilliant!).

But my journal is more than a record of my disease. It serves as a place in which I can record my feelings—my fears, hopes, disappointments. In it I note the details of the life that surrounds me—the birds that come to the feeder, the names of the books I read, the nuances of the seasons. I record conversations with friends, private thoughts, and crazy ideas. I treasure my journal; it is like a friend that I can turn to daily.

In this book I have quoted many portions of my journal. These excerpts illuminate the idea or feeling I am trying to convey in the text. Because they were written close to the moment of the experience, my journal entries give expression to life with cancer that is immediate, honest, and sometimes raw. (Entries on similar subjects, but written on different days, are separated by an ornament.) I hope that the use of my journal in this book adds to your understanding of the difficult time you are engaged in. I also hope it encourages you to keep a journal as well. It is an effective tool for the journey.

❧ Part One ❧
Diagnosis and Adjustment

But those who wait on the Lord
Shall renew their strength;
They shall mount up with wings like eagles,
They shall run and not be weary,
They shall walk and not faint.

—Isaiah 40:31 (KJV)

As you adjust to living with a life-threatening disease, what lies heavily on your mind? What are your concerns, your fears, your worries? What are your hopes, your wishes? The purpose of this book is to deal as honestly as possible with these issues, and to share the thoughts and experiences of someone who is traveling the same path that you are.

Part one is organized around the various stages you will go through as you adjust to your new circumstances. It may seem that you should go through each individual stage before moving on to the next—this is not the way it goes! Rather, we go "backing and forthing" throughout our journey. We can go from gloom to glory in a matter of minutes, just as we can go from calm to panic and back again in no time at all. But as we become accustomed to our disease, we will spend less time in the pit and more time loving the life we have. Honest.

DIAGNOSIS

I will begin at the beginning, the day of diagnosis.

A call from the doctor. Bad news. I have been given my chance at life. I'm fifty-two. I didn't paint those pictures or write those books or become great at anything. But I did raise three wonderful and remarkable children. I have known love and terrible loss. I have known joy, agony, anger, bliss, contentment, resentment, passion, peace, fear, ecstasy, longing, loneliness. I have experienced the full range of feelings. Now I feel a little afraid, alone—because no one can travel the path that lies before me with me. Well, so be it. I will try to get my affairs in order. I will try to find some comfort, maybe some hope, and hope I have enough courage.

For many of us, the news sends us into shock. We can hardly fathom the seriousness of our situation. We are numb. And that is lucky, I think. We have a time of unreality that lets bits and pieces of ourselves get used to the idea of our very changed circumstances. I remember going to the grocery store and wondering what I was doing there. And how could others be going about their business, talking and laughing and checking prices, as though life was the same as usual? Life was not the same as usual, and it never will be. At least that is how it seems.

Tips for survival:
- Go to the grocery store. You still have to eat.
- Buy a journal. Today. And start writing. Write anything, but write.

- Go to a really funny movie and laugh out loud, even if no one else is laughing.
- Watch where you walk. Look both ways before crossing a street. (Remember, you're numb.)

DENIAL

Denial is another helpful device, and is a stage in itself. Denial allows us to go on with our daily lives, regardless of how shattered we may feel at other times. In denial, we say, "This can't be happening to me." Or, "The lab must have made a mistake." Or, "It can't be that bad." Denial is a good coping mechanism. Don't scorn it. But don't let it prevent you from getting treatment or taking care of yourself. And we can't live in denial for long because . . . the pit hits.

Am I not facing reality? I wonder. If I refuse to face reality, I think I can change reality. If I laugh in the face of disaster, it will change its face. Maybe I refuse to acknowledge cancer's potential to kill me, because if I admitted its power, it would kill me. Ah, perhaps I'm just an optimist, and perhaps an optimist is always a bit of a liar.

Family and friends often enter into denial with us. Denial may even prevent them from helping us when we most need it. Or denial may make them diminish the seriousness of our situation, and they may encourage us to believe that everything will be okay. But denial does not mean that they don't love us; they wouldn't be in denial if they didn't love us.

When in denial:

- Go to the grocery store now if you didn't make it before.
- Buy a pair of winter boots or sandals— whichever is out of season.
- Plant a tree.
- Keep writing—try for at least ten minutes daily.
- Pinch yourself and say aloud, "This is my life!"
- Enjoy the respite.

*T*HE PIT

The pit, I suppose, is useful, too. In any case, it is a place that we all go and do not enjoy. The pit is awful. And it has many dimensions: terror, loneliness, despair, anxiety, hopelessness, anger.

We need God. We need to have God exist. There is nothing without God. Emptiness. Terror. Isolation. Meaninglessness. I am truly thankful I have read Camus, Sartre, even Hemingway before now. If I thought I was the first to think or experience these ideas, I'd go mad. I am sometimes terrified as I look at my reality, but then I pull back, remember God and my family and feel a measure of safety and sense once again—and then I force myself to refuse looking into that awfulness again. I cannot bear more than a glimpse.

✣

Sometimes I can't think too much or all meaning falls apart. Life, my life, others' lives, seem pointless, frail, empty, lonely. We clutch one another, our jobs, our routines, God, because the despair and desperation are just on the other side of the veil. And then I weep—for my children, whom I want to protect from such feelings. I want them to experience joy, utter abandonment, and the deliciousness of life. But I know they, at such young ages, know the taste, that dreadful ache, of pain. They know it too soon.

Yes, a sense of panic and fear can come rushing our way when we feel we are losing our foothold in life. Bravado frequently works to allay those fears, but the possibility of hopelessness and despair march alongside and can arrest us at any moment. We do so much to ward off the terror: we work, we reshuffle papers, we immerse ourselves in activity, in noise, in problems; we seek reassurance in books, art, music, friends, family, and church. We keep busy. Often our busyness is good, certainly. Meaningful work is wonderful; daily tasks are a gift to each of us, but perhaps most needed and at the core of our needs is love. Amazing. Love that pours unbidden is the love that astounds us and fills us with joy and eases our fears.

But even as we gain a measure of control over our fears, we are thrown off-balance by other dynamics: our moods careen wildly, and even reality itself seems unstable.

Odd. Odd. Life is too odd. Hope, nothing, exhilaration, a sense of doom are so closely interwoven. Feverish despair. Futility mixed with determination. I will overcome. But why? I'll yield, but no. There is a design in this chaos. Or is there chaos in this design? Regardless, time never stops.

And, sometimes, it seems that our own death comes to us in bits and pieces—sometimes in flashes. Death, too, is odd.

✣

Life leaps along, and not in a straight path. I plunge into infinite emptiness, infinite possibilities; shuddering hope and lostness struggle back and forth. I am fascinated, fearful, so terribly aware! Life is so very uncertain.

And then there is anger. We ask ourselves why this had to happen now (as though there is any perfect time to get a disease!), just when things were going so well for us. Or perhaps we feel we have already had our share of suffering and pain. This is just not fair. Or we blame God. How could a loving God allow this to happen? (This question requires another book.) In the meantime, what we are really asking is, "Why me?" Perhaps a better, more productive question is, "Why not me?" So many have afflictions of one sort or another, what's so special about me that I should escape?

In another dark corner of the pit, loneliness lurks. In the middle of the night, in a bustling store, while raking leaves, or even in the presence of friends, a wave of utter loneliness can strike.

My heart is lonely, my candle of hope is dim indeed. I am alone, I'm weary, and in this weariness I gather myself to myself and find a measure of peace and comfort. Tomorrow I hope to look outward. God be with me in this lonely stretch of life.

Tips for getting through the pit:

- Call a friend from your distant past.

- Give someone a present.

- Take a long, aromatic bath.

- Keep a basket filled with cards and letters from friends. Read them.

- Clean a drawer, a cupboard, a closet.

- Listen to lively music. Dance.

Glimmers of Light

Strangely enough, the most difficult moments are so often tinged with beauty. As we become acquainted with the depths and the darkest corners of life, we can also be enabled to see and treasure the glimmers of light—our families, our friends, a good meal, chickadees at the bird feeder, an apple tree heavy with blooms.

I like being here by myself with my silent, heavy-footed cat. I am so glad to be here in my cozy house, to be alive, to be able. Life! Life! I love life. I don't want to lose it. It's so short. The good years are few. But richness surrounds me, even in the midst of pain. Oh, I ache. I yearn. I'm filled to overflowing. My heart bursts. Love, joy, pain, sorrow. They're all there, mixed into something that says, "My cup runneth over."

ᴥ

I want to live! I want to live! And, oh, how I thrive on fun. I'll never outgrow my love of fun, but will I die too soon?

Will eternal life be fun? I never picture it as fun! And, Lord, I love fun and I love to laugh. And I thank God for laughter, for friends, for fellow laughers! I don't want to die. I don't even want to be sick, though I'll put up with sickness. But I'll never not want laughter. I celebrate laughter!

❧

Life forces struggle with death forces. I yearn toward life. CT scans thorax, abdomen, and pelvis—searching out death forces. My senses explode with life.

❧

Life ebbs and flows. Nothing is constant, nothing sure. Life is such a scary gift!

Loss, Change, Relinquishment

The losses we face are perhaps a less frightening part of the pit, but they are certainly a difficult reality to come to terms with. The biggest loss is our health, but with that come many other losses.

I will never again be a young woman who feels like a girl. I'm a different person than I was before all this business began. The romantic optimist that I was makes me smile now—and smile fondly—it was a lovely way to live!

❧

I grieve. I grieve over little things that are gone. I can hardly bear to think of the past, and yet it is such a dear treasure to me. Youth, innocence, ease—gone! I'm not young anymore, and the change happened so suddenly, so decisively. Cancer has zapped my zest, my innocent joy, hope, and confidence.

And in that former life, one of our gifts was that we could take life for granted. We could take our role in life for granted. And, yes, others could take us for granted and we could take those we love for granted. All of that is gone, but until it is gone, we don't realize what a gift it was! In its place comes a new awareness and a new appreciation of those around us, of nature, of our very breath. But we can no longer assume that life is ours, and that is a loss; both for us and for those who love us.

I am stripped of so much, I am defenseless. I can only feel the sun on my face and laugh, laugh with the whole of my being! I surrender to what is, take it into my being, and revel in the crumbs of life. Thanks be to God for these shreds and shards of life—the bits that sear and the bits that flow and embrace me. My hair falls in bits onto this page, onto my pillow, onto my shoulders, onto my rugs, into the drain, onto my food—my hair sheds, more life leaves. But there is always the hope of restoration, of renewal.

We also need to relinquish some of the plans, hopes, and dreams for our lives. Many of us have to be near our healthcare providers regularly, and our energy is diminished. Long trips, new jobs, and moving to new locations may not be options for us.

I wish I could wander with my daughter, sit on tops of mountains and talk about dreams, ghosts, and guardian

*angels. I wish I could paddle down silent streams with her
and listen to mysterious calls from deep within the woods,
and I wish I could shout truths from beneath waterfalls
and she, with water cascading down her, could bubble
with laughter and be filled with her light.*

Physically, we may lose our hair, our appetites,
our energy. We may gain weight or lose weight. We
may become weaker. We may not be able to work as
we once did. How can we handle all these changes?

I remember those first mornings after I was
home from the hospital when I could hear the neigh-
bors' cars start up for the morning commute. And I
was still in bed. I felt lonely, guilty, cut off from so
much of life. Now I savor those free mornings!
Instead of rushing off to work, I have my morning
coffee, read the paper, take a luxuriously warm, aromatic bath, go for a walk with a friend, and have the
freedom to create much of the rest of my day. So, new
opportunities are available to us. We have to be open
to them and, in fact, look for them.

Our physical changes challenge us also. One
evening, I was sitting at the dinner table with my son,
Seth, and his college roommate, Jeshua. I was a bit
downhearted. Another series of treatments was
about to begin, and I told the boys I dreaded losing
my hair for the fourth time. I was tired of being a
freak. Jeshua reached over to me, grabbed my hand
and said, "But we love you, Freak!" And then I was
fine. Love is much more important than a head of
hair! (Laughter helped, too.)

Yes, humor does help. Shortly after I first lost my hair, my family and I were at our cabin. I was sitting on the deck, watching the hummingbirds zoom to and from the feeder, when my ninety-five year old father came up behind me, drew a line across my totally bald head, and said, "You know, you don't look bad this way, but have you ever thought of parting it on the other side?"

That same summer a friend from Texas dropped by the cabin. As we were visiting on the deck, my sister complained about her hair which is long and thick, and that day was also frizzy and matted. She said, "Uff, I just don't know what to do with this awful hair!" Sig looked at her, then at me, and back at her. "Have you ever considered trying chemo?" he asked.

My life is utterly changed! And through these massive changes what has happened to me? Am I different? Perhaps. I have certainly learned much about myself, life, prayer, people, and the power of love and laughter. And I have discovered that throughout my deepest grief, my anguish, my illness, the experiences of sublime peace, love, tenderness, and goodness have been ever available to me. Thanks be to God.

✧

Life changes can drastically alter our plans, our chosen paths. All of a sudden what we thought was our life is no longer. It's the "before and after" syndrome—before the war, after the war; before the children, after the children; before the accident, after the accident; before the divorce, after the divorce; before major illness, after major illness; and, of course, before a loved one dies and after a loved one dies. We all experience changes in our lives—sometimes welcome changes, sometimes brutal changes. And we are affected and life is never the same as it was before.

Tips for surviving changes:
- If your hair begins to falls out, vacuum your head daily.
- Journal about your changes.
- Laugh about your situation; encourage others to laugh with you.

Coming to Terms

As we let go and accept our new situation, life shifts. We reawaken with new perceptions, new priorities, and even a different sense of time.

Letting go. What a huge part of life that is, but so often I haven't realize what a large ingredient it is. I always thought I could recover a neglected friendship, retrieve wasted time, return to a former situation. Life seemed to go slowly and stay the same for huge blocks of time. Not so now. I am so aware of what I have, and what I have lost. And the losses make what I have seem so very precious— because I will lose it—will lose everything—life itself— I will lose even this moment when I lie here on my couch so contentedly with my music, my journal, my dear little house, and, oh so soon, I'll lose the presence of my dear son who is sitting at the dining room table, reading. All of this will go. My journal will be full, this late Sunday night music will give way to daytime music and news. My house will belong to someone else as it belonged to the Hawkinsons before me, and my life in it will be over. And Seth will leave and very likely never return to really live here again. But this moment I love, and in it I find deep contentment. Contentment is my companion.

One perception that becomes so real to us is that life is a delicate balance between hope and despair, courage and fear, dread and longing.

We live on the fine edge of sadness and hope, and I teeter from one to the other. I know hope is a great gift and I know life has enormous sadness. I experience both daily. The day is gray and chilly, but friends and family surround me and this melancholy moment can change into a burst of joy so quickly, so easily—so neither the dark nor the light is permanent.

Hope! What a strangely important ingredient in our lives! It's absolutely essential, in fact. Without hope, life seems pointless. Despair is our true enemy.

I'm always pushing. Perhaps I am afraid of stillness—my fears, dreads, apprehensions, sadness, aloneness surface and break my fighting spirit, my hope, my optimism, my fragile, delicately balanced hope and optimism. Ah, how quickly and deeply I can plunge into despair and utter

sadness. But for now, my life is full; I feel courage surge within me—and how I want to live!

✤

Joy is wrung out of suffering. It is the star in a black night. It doesn't dispel the darkness—it illuminates it, it contrasts with it, it is in it.

Sometimes we key into new perceptions in unusual ways. A dream, a talk with someone we love, a long walk alone, and writing in our journals can all lead us to some insight about our new lives.

A dream: I dreamt that I was in a large auditorium speaking to a huge crowd with both familiar and unfamiliar faces, and I was concerned about getting my lipstick on dark enough, and then I lost my notes for the speech. I tried to collect my thoughts, but my written speech had gone clean out of my mind! When I got up to speak I had a new story to tell. And I told about the seasonal changes as I drove back and forth to Mayo Clinic, and I spoke about the new country I had moved to, the country of cancer. I spoke about my doctor with his warm soul who cared for my body and my spirit, my loving nurse who became my trusted friend, and the bond between those of us with cancer. And this new country was not my chosen land, but it, too, had its riches and rewards—for example, the time I spend traveling under a big sky, watching the rolling fields with their changing colors: black, bare soil followed by tender green shoots that grow into tall, dark, green corn, which ripen to a golden tan, and in time the harvested fields are full of stubble, and finally, before it all begins again, the covering of deep white snow. And then I awakened and said, "Yes, this is my new country and it is good."

Tips to encourage us to accept:
- Acknowledge that life remains mysterious.
- Begin each day with a prayer of thanksgiving.
- Remember, we all live until we die. So live.
- Look for the beauty surrounding you.

$\mathcal{A}$DAPTATION AND PURPOSE

As we adapt to our new situation, often we feel the need to find a new purpose for our lives. What is truly important for us to do with the time and energy we have? I suppose we need to find our mission, our calling.

I need to give the life I have been given. Where? Doing what? I don't know except that I must give wherever I find myself, doing whatever I am doing. I don't want my life to be so small. Is this pride, zeal, stupidity, an altogether natural reaction to all I've been through? Probably all of the above.

Oh, my life, my life. Emotions bombard me. And I'm here—alone in my sanctuary. Dear God, thank you and lead me. I want so to hear where my next step should lead. Give me life and grace, and the strength to bear all things. My life, life itself, is short and dear. Odd how we all struggle to keep it going! The duration, whether forty or ninety years, is so short! I guess we just want to live long enough to feel like we have seen enough, done enough, loved

enough. Have I come close to becoming the person God intended me to become?

Sometimes a purpose is so very commonplace we almost miss it.

I was feeling worthless because I had to focus so much on my health when a call from my son reassured me. He said my fight was important to him and to the other children because I was the magnet that kept them together; I was "home." I will continue to fight!

Surely one thing we can do is live our lives as richly and as well as we are able. We can notice and participate in the wealth of life that surrounds us.

Ah, that cancer. It's like a shadow I can never get away from. I guess none of this will end before I do. Well, I'll live as best I can, as fully as I can, until I no longer can. Oh my. I'll collect little precious fragments of life every day; I'll perceive the sheer beauty of the dot on which I stand! This moment, for example, even as it's laced with some grim realities—realities of cancer, ringing ears, vision problems, numb toes, aching neck—is still beautiful in the absolute stillness of this room, the green plants growing, thriving, the sheen of the wood floors, the serious, handsome wooden doors, cupboards, window frames, the comfort and security of such an honest and sturdy house. And I could play music! read a book! write a friend! Possibilities are here!

Tips for finding purpose and living meaningfully:

- Make a list of things you want to do before you die. Start doing them.
- Be hospitable.
- Pray for direction.
- Take advantage of opportunities to serve.
- Use your energy wisely.
- Be as active as your health permits.
- If you were to die in a week, what would be your regrets? Can you do anything about those regrets?
- Live boldly. It may be your last chance.

❧ *Part Two* ❧
Treatment and Beyond

Out of my distress I called on the Lord;
the Lord answered and set me free.
With the Lord on my side I do not fear.
                                    —Psalm 118:5-6

❧

The second part of this book deals with issues regarding treatment, life after treatment, recurrence (which I hope you will not have to know about!), and what it is like to live with the reality of death.

TREATMENT

> I lift up my eyes to the hills.
> From whence does my help come?
> My help comes from the Lord,
> who made heaven and earth.
> He will not let your foot be moved,
> he who keeps you will not slumber.
> Behold, he who keeps Israel
> will neither slumber nor sleep.
> The Lord is your keeper;
> the Lord is your shade on your right hand.
> The sun shall not smite you by day,
> nor the moon by night.
> The Lord will keep you from all evil;
> he will keep your life.
> The Lord will keep
> your going out and your coming in
> from this time forth and for evermore.
>
> —Psalm 121

For most of us, some sort of treatment is imperative if we want to continue living. And that treatment is often, though not always, tough to handle. Some treatments are worse than others, and everyone handles treatment differently. Generally, however, many of today's treatments cause some unpleasant side-effects. We may experience nausea, hair loss, numbing of fingers and toes, joint pain, bone aches, a deep-down weariness; our blood counts may plunge. Often we feel like we have the flu. These side-effects are not fun. And yet we continue to submit our bodies to poisons, drugs, radiation. We do this because we hope to cure or, at least, to control our disease. We need the treatment. We dread it. But we do it. It is an odd situation, but through it all we come to realize more profoundly the gift that life is.

I'm waiting for treatment and I hear the murmur of voices, someone coughing, isolated words: "Chemo . . . make it positive for you . . . Yes, it was changed." Words of patients mingle with words from the staff behind the desk. We're all polite, civil; we smile as we are led off to our bit of torture, our doses of poison. How odd, really!

One of the difficulties of treatment is that we know beforehand what it is we face. We never know when other illnesses might strike, so we don't tend to anticipate them. Not so with these treatments! We come to know and value that we, for the most part, don't know the future, and that this lack of knowledge is a gift. Often throughout life we have been anxious to know how things will turn out—things like our children's lives, our careers, a romance, a test score. Now we learn that we should just love the day for what it has to offer.

Tomorrow begins a five-day stint of treatment, and that depresses me. I dread all that. I need to keep putting one foot in front of the other, one foot in front of the other— don't look ahead and don't look behind. Just keep on keeping on. I just want less of life slamming doors as it seems to be doing right now. But life changes. Nothing stays the same and soon my spirits will once again soar.

But sometimes treatment isn't so bad. In fact, sometimes it can be, at least partly, pleasant.

I'm at the hospital—and loving it! The food is so good, the room is pleasant, the nurses wonderful. I've been thinking of this whole treatment business as a job, but what a pleasant job it sometimes is. The down side is when they draw blood—I feel like a human pin cushion. But today no blood work. So I sip my coffee, eat my doughnut and orange, and feel spoiled! Now I have a couple of hours to read and write. Again the sky is blue, a hint of fall is in the air, in the leaves which are just beginning to turn. The view from my window makes me happy.

How much should we know about our treatments? Should we know the potential side-effects, both immediate and long-term? Should we learn the names of our medications? Should we keep track of our reactions? Should we investigate and learn about other treatments for our disease? The answers are fairly individual, but we need to consider very carefully how much knowledge we need in order to feel that we can most fully participate in our healing.

I can't control everything, but the more I know and the more I feel a measure of control over my own situation, the better I like it. So give me the reports, teach me about the meds, the side effects; don't spare me.

On the other hand, I think it is important that we don't simply become our disease. We need to take care of ourselves, but we also need to nourish the parts of us that are healthy.

I don't spend a lot of time thinking about my cancer. Somehow to focus on that seems to be giving in to it. I prefer a less direct fight—maximize the rest of my life and minimize the role of cancer in my life. Yes, I'll devote Wednesdays to it because I must, but for as long as possible the other six days belong to the rest of my life.

Sometimes, however, the treatment so diminishes the quality of our lives that we wonder if life will ever be "normal" again.

Will I ever feel energy pouring through me again? Will little jobs cease looking difficult? I have a load of clothes to get out of the dryer and fold, and even that seems hard! But I still enjoy reading, spending time with my family, writing, savoring my morning cups of tea, crawling into my cozy bed, looking around a clean house, eating good food, going for drives, thinking, remembering, talking to friends. Oh, so much I enjoy, and really this day is good. Of course, I dread some things in the future. Where is my life going? Just a march to death?

Tips for surviving treatment:
- Get prepared before treatment. Clean your house, do the laundry, mow the yard, wash and gas the car, shop for groceries, make food that can be frozen and warmed later, pay the bills. Then, when you are lying around feeling perfectly useless, you won't feel guilty!

- When others offer to help, think of specific things they could do for you.

- Ask for help if you need it.

- If you are concerned about your reaction to treatment, call your doctor or nurse.

- Journal about your reactions to treatment. You may need to tell your doctor about those side-effects.

- Make a list of questions that you have before you see your doctor.

- Ask a friend or relative to go with you to see your doctor. It is difficult to remember everything the doctor says, especially when you hear something that affects you emotionally. Have your friend or relative take notes for you to refer to later.

- If possible, talk to someone else having the same treatment you are; you can compare notes and reassure one another.

- Consider joining a support group.

- Stay away from people who depress or upset you.

- Stay away from people who have a cold or the flu.

- Remember, getting well is your number one job right now. Do your best.

- Rest whenever you need to.

- Eat nutritiously. Surround yourself with good cooks!

- Prevent nausea. It's tough once it has gotten a grip.

- Exercise. Try to remain active, but don't push yourself too hard.

- Try to speak openly about your illness so others will be at ease with you. Sometimes people are afraid they will offend you or upset you if they mention your illness. It is our job to get rid of that barrier in our relationships.

- Investigate therapies such as massage, meditation, guided imagery, art therapy, acupuncture, yoga, herbal medicine, homeopathy. Try them. (Make sure they will not interfere with your conventional treatment.)

- Find opportunities to laugh and have fun.

- As my wise doctor says, don't be a wimp!

- Pray for healing.

- Find prayer warriors and solicit their prayers.

LIFE AFTER TREATMENT

> Thou hast delivered my soul from death,
> my eyes from tears,
> my feet from stumbling;
> I walk before the Lord
> in the land of the living.
> What shall I render to the Lord
> for all his bounty to me?
>
> —Psalm 116:8-9, 12

Finally the day comes when we finish our treatments. This is truly a day to celebrate, and yet anxieties often arise when we don't have the treatment to rely on to fight our disease. The treatments, we realize, have made us feel more secure and safe.

It's the morning of my last (and I pray that it is my last) chemo. My taste buds and stomach are already revolting. I long for this day to be over! Then four or five days of worthlessness and then!! Oh, be quiet, my eager heart. I do need to allow my feelings and then deal with them productively. I'm so afraid that any negative feelings will cause me to have more cancer! But I can't stay on the crest of the wave forever. There are hard realities that I need to face. Living presents its own set of problems!

What will life after treatment be like? Indeed, we discover that we need to adjust once again. Our schedule for treatment is gone! Our doctor's appointments are infrequent. We feel our energy return, and as our energy returns we become more confident that we can return to a fairly normal life. Now we need to examine our former activities and obligations. Have our priorities changed, and are we listening to what we have learned? Or are we just going to slip back into our old ways and forget the hard-won lessons that we were so certain would change us forever?

How have we changed? I hope we are more aware of the details of life around us, the moment, the small fluxes of life. I hope we hold life and those we love more tenderly and fully. I hope we can find our place in the universe and I hope we can walk more humbly on our earth, with our God and with our fellow travelers. Finally, I hope we can grow in wisdom as long as we live.

I feel that thing called hope tug at my heart once again. Life continues to call to me; I am intrigued, hopeful, and still am foolish enough to believe in magic and mystery, in love and truth and beauty, and I hope I will grab life with gusto and not spend too much time daydreaming.

Tips for life after treatment:

- Celebrate! Have a party or let someone throw a party for you.
- Write out a list of your priorities. What, specifically, do you want to do with this new life? What are your goals? What steps do you need to take to accomplish them?
- Journal about your experience as you adjust.
- Thank God daily for your life and health.

*R*ECURRENCE

> I cry to thee, O Lord;
> I say, Thou art my refuge,
> my portion in the land of the living.
> Give heed to my cry;
> for I am brought very low!
> —Psalm 142:5-6

Sometimes after we have fought a long and hard battle against our disease and we are savoring our freedom from having to deal with illness, a routine doctor visit dashes our spirits once again. We have that dreaded recurrence. For many this news is more difficult to bear than the original diagnosis was. We've already worked so hard to get well! We've already endured pain and suffering; can we go through all that again? Must we?

The day is bright and cold, intensely cold. Clear, deep blue skies are reflected in the mounds of fresh, clean snow. On this glorious morning, the news is not good. My cancer is back. I guess I won't get off so easily after all. I feel numb and I ache. How lucky I was feeling! I thought a whole new life might open before me. But now it looks like I'll just have to dig in and endure and fight for my life again. I'll set my hopes and dreams aside, get my life in order and get myself ready to go into battle again. I'm so disappointed. But it's just my life at risk, not the purpose and meaning of my life, so it is bearable.

I awakened with a start—the cancer scare startle that so often jolts me into wakefulness. I don't like this experience. I've been here before. It's a period of adjustment, of getting reacquainted with my mortality, up close and personal. It's being overwhelmed by jobs, by routes to take. I need to just take the reins and go where I want to go. But today I just can't manage the burden of sorrow, the work, my tiredness, the thought of activity, obligations. Even feeding myself nutritiously seems a burden. I'm low. But I'll be all right. I've been down this road before and I've always found my way to brightness, and I will, I will. But now I mourn. And I beg God to heal me. But for what? My life feels too useless to me, at least today. I feel immersed in things I don't want, and detached from those I long for. Oh, I'm just at a standstill right now, too dismayed to

move on, but I will get used to my new reality and life will go on.

❧

Where will I find the strength and will to go on? Will my body be able to take this next onslaught of chemo? It is hard to bear all that I have to face. I try to keep my spirits up, but, oh my! I yearn for ease, but I know I can do what I need to do, whatever that may be.

Eventually, we adjust to this news, too. Yes, we weep and long for ease, but we keep going and, in time, some of us, because we must, begin to think of our disease as chronic. Along the way we come to terms with the realization that we just have to continue treating it and hope that our bodies can endure the drugs, CT scans, MRIs, and radiation (and that our doctors won't run out of treatment options for us).

I don't feel as vulnerable now, even though I am repeating my last year's ordeal. The drama and fear are gone, or at least greatly diminished, and I feel more able to handle my situation—less needy, less fragile, less lonely. This time around I feel more independent, and more like I am the one fighting the battle. It was such a group effort last time. Now the support is still there, but the energy level is down. My supporters are a more subdued band of people. I just hope their prayers are as fervent.

❧

My cancer is now an integral part of my life, a part of the rhythm of my life. Chemo on a regular schedule, followed by predictable "down days," and then two weeks of glorious health. I mark my calendar in anticipation of these events.

❧

I can't imagine a "cancer-free" life anymore. How would my plans, my hopes be different if I didn't have cancer? Where would I be working? Would I have put off traveling, teaching abroad? Would I be living in this house?

Tips for surviving a recurrence:

- Allow yourself to weep. Finding out that your disease has recurred is devastating.

- The day you learn about the recurrence, plan an evening out, doing something you love to do. Dress up and go to a play, a concert, dinner, or at least go to a funny movie. (The afternoon I learned of my third recurrence, some friends happened to call me and invite me to dinner and the theater. We spent a splendid summer evening at the Guthrie Theater in Minneapolis. This lovely memory is enhanced because of the contrast to the day's miserable news.)

- Talk to others who have experienced a recurrence and survived.

- Seek the best medical advice and treatment program available to you.

- Continue to pray for healing; for physical, emotional, and spiritual wholeness.

Facing Our Mortality

> Yea, though I walk through the valley
> of the shadow of death,
> I will fear no evil;
> For You are with me.
>
> —Psalm 23:4 (KJV)

As we live with a life-threatening disease, we also live with a keener sense of our own mortality. Sometimes the very real presence of death is frightening; sometimes it puts life into sharp focus; sometimes it fills us with a sense of urgency.

My doctor said, essentially, I would probably live less than a year. Yet every part of me tingles with life! But, I will breathe the breath of life more deeply now. I will try to live more fully, not more busily, but more aware.

I'm in this cancer thing now and time is not on my side. I need to do with my life what I want to have done. I need to live fully. I sometimes feel a twinge of fright at what is coming, but I quickly jump back in the present where I'm safe—or into the past that is so bittersweet. The present is the best place for me to be these days, but the past lingers with me, a shadow companion, and the future path opens before I want to get there—a glimpse is all I dare take. And even the present is tinged with melancholy because it slips away moment by moment and it, too, is lost and gone.

Sometimes I sense, feel, taste my own death. And a certain—terror? panic?—arises within me. Other times I feel so utterly alone. And sometimes that aloneness gives me strength, boldness, maybe even pride, but other times that aloneness makes me feel so empty, so isolated.

❧

So much to do, so little time! Once again my vulnerability asserts itself; this time I feel a lump in my neck. Is this my last fall? I feel more vulnerable than I think I ever have, but I also feel calm, at least I have so far. I'm not giving up, but—what—I'm not sure. I guess I feel more accepting, less fearful than I have in the past.

Even though we are aware of the very real threat that disease presents to our lives, many of us dig our heels into life with greater tenacity than ever before. But even as we are doing this, we are aware of both the courage and the ridiculousness of such spirit. Nonetheless, we continue to choose life, even when the obstacles become huge.

My friend Carole called last night. Her cancer has gone to her brain now. She uses a walker, slurs her words a bit, and is facing radiation followed by chemotherapy. When I mentioned "terminal," she said she's not ready for that yet. It is amazing how we adjust to our reduced circumstances and continue to want life even though living becomes increasingly difficult for us and for everyone around us. The human spirit is amazing, I think.

❧

Oh, Life! How we work to sustain it—and, in the end, we die anyway. Sometimes I wonder about the sense of it all.

Odd how life is—so short and finally we are so utterly helpless. So utterly alone and helpless. We do need God.

I long to run and jump with that sweet sense of well-being that I used to know. I want to dart around instead of plod along. Perhaps that is what heaven is like, and why old and sick people yearn for it. What they really want is the good part of their lives—the laughter, the ease, the sense of accomplishment, the warmth of love and loving. Yes, the promise to wipe away all tears, get rid of all pain—inside and outside—and to bask in the sunlight of life. Death is such a mystery. I dread mostly the agony of getting there and leaving life and my loved ones behind. And I am not happy about relinquishing the future!

As we ponder the possible brevity of our lives, we may also have some regrets. Some of those regrets we need to let go; others we may yet overcome or correct. Regardless, we do need to live the rest of our lives the way we want them lived. This is our last chance to do it right!

My time looks short. At odd moments I hear a song, see a picture, think of distant places or strenuous physical activities and wham! My life feels like it's shutting down. Regrets? Of course! I wish I had gone more places, had more adventures, learned more, done more creative work. But I have had a good life. I've had wonderful friends, children, family, good jobs, and nice homes. I've paddled down rivers, been to Paris and London, I've read good books, eaten delicious food, held my babies for hours and hours. I've watched sunsets, meteor showers, I've inhaled every season's aroma. I've listened to operas, chamber music, and cicadas and bull frogs. I've sung hymns, laughed, wept. Yes, I weep.

Life slips by so quickly. How many books will remain unread! How many thoughts unsaid! I love my little house. I love the order, the peace, the music, my cozy office. I'm okay for now. Thank you, God, for the peace I have. But now I will turn off the lights, the music, turn down the heat, and go upstairs. The house is empty, silent. I am here. I am here.

Some of our concerns regarding death are very prosaic. I remember awakening with a start in the middle of the night shortly after surgery. I was certain my children would never find anything in my jumbled files. Their inheritance would be lost! So, as part of our mental recovery, we need to take the time to get things in order—our wills, our files, our banking, our deeds. We need to clean our drawers, our closets, our cupboards, and throw out anything we don't want to burden others with—or have them find. Once we have gotten ready to die, we can relax into life.

Even as we face our mortality, it is important to keep a sense of humor. Several years ago I asked my local doctor—a gruff, shy, brilliant surgeon—how long I could expect to live. He told me that statistically people in my situation did well to live five years. I asked him when that five years began—now? When I had the surgery? When I was diagnosed? He said most counted from the time of diagnosis. I was shocked. That gave me just a few more months to live! I countered by saying that my friend Marlene was still alive with worse cancer than mine and she had had it for twelve years. His response? "She ought to be dead, too!" And we laughed and laughed.

ℱACING THE FUTURE

The Lord answer you in the day of trouble!
The name of the God of Jacob protect you!
May he grant you your heart's desire,
and fulfil all your plans!
May we shout for joy over your victory,
and in the name of our God set up our banners!
May the Lord fulfil all your petitions!

—Psalm 20:1, 4, 5

Finally, we can't know the future, but we can prepare ourselves for our journey through life. We can arm ourselves with love, faith, hope, grace, and courage. We can pray for our lives to be long, our souls to be comforted, our words and deeds to be good.

I am in another reality, indeed another dimension on some days. I am looking at life through slitted eyes, eyes that often travel beyond this day, the present plan, the next holiday. I'm not yet sure what I see. Perhaps that will become clearer as I travel this length of road. For now I know this day was both dark and light and that at this moment, as I sit here, wrapped in cozy blankets, cross-legged on my bed at 11:00 at night, I feel peace and I feel safe and I thank God for this day and pray for another. In the meantime, the lumps on my neck remain, I think of burial plans, executors, house deed, and wills. And that is okay, too. Though now, when I feel so much better, I want to live a long, long time!

> For you shall go out in joy,
> and be led forth in peace;
> the mountains and the hills before you
> shall break forth into singing,
> and all the trees of the field shall clap their hands.
> —Isaiah 55:12

✤

Other Resources from Augsburg

When You Are Facing a Divorce
by Jan Jovaag Ansorge
48 pages, ISBN 0-8066-4361-7

This book addresses individuals who
are learning to live with the life-altering
decision of divorce.

Psalms for Healing
by Gretchen Person
170 pages, ISBN 0-8066-4161-4

A thoughtful collection of psalms and
prayers for those who seek healing.

Finding the Right Words
by Wilfred Bockelman
80 pages, ISBN 0-8066-2444-2

This helpful book gives practical suggestions for offering care and comfort. The
author discusses many common situations
and provides help for knowing what to say.

Available wherever books are sold.
To order these books directly, contact:
1-800-328-4648 • www.augsburgfortress.org
Augsburg Fortress, Publishers
P.O. Box 1209, Minneapolis, MN 55440-1209